GENETICS

by Christine Petersen

Content Consultant
Nancy Cox
Section Chief for the Section of Genetic Medicine in the
Department of Medicine, University of Chicago

CORE
LIBRARY

Published by ABDO Publishing Company, PO Box 398166, Minneapolis, MN 55439. Copyright © 2014 by Abdo Consulting Group, Inc. International copyrights reserved in all countries. No part of this book may be reproduced in any form without written permission from the publisher. The Core Library™ is a trademark and logo of ABDO Publishing Company.

Printed in the United States of America,
North Mankato, Minnesota
102013
012014

♻ THIS BOOK CONTAINS AT LEAST 10% RECYCLED MATERIALS.

Editor: Arnold Ringstad
Series Designer: Becky Daum

Library of Congress Cataloging-in-Publication Data
Petersen, Christine, author.
  Genetics / by Christine Petersen ; content consultant Nancy Cox.
     pages cm. -- (The science of life)
  Audience: 8 to 12.
  Includes bibliographical references.
  ISBN 978-1-62403-161-8
1. Genetics--Juvenile literature. 2. DNA--Juvenile literature. I. Title.
  QH437.5.P48 2014
  576.5--dc23
                           2013031908

CONTENTS

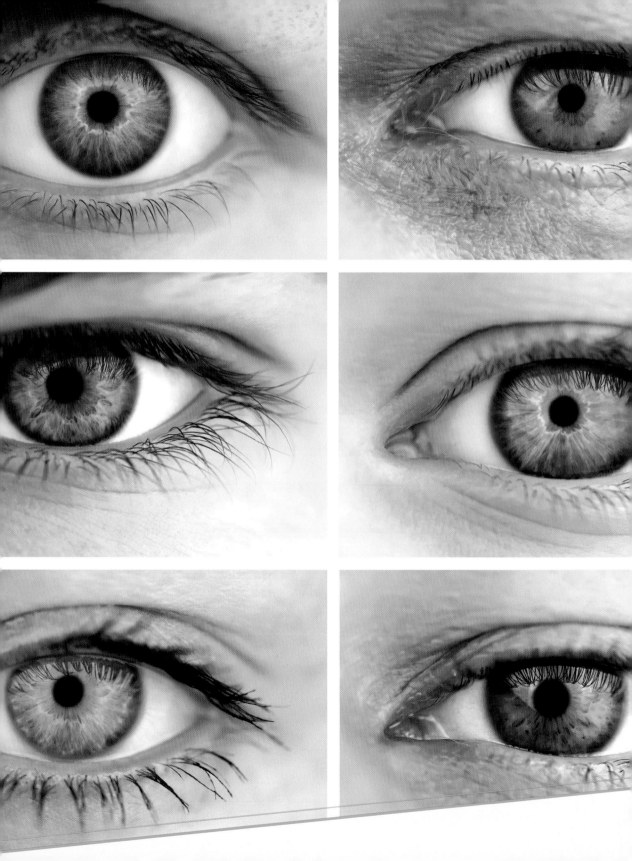

CHAPTER ONE

TRACKING TRAITS

Have you ever heard that you look like family members? There are good reasons for this. Children inherit features such as hair, eye, and skin color from their parents. These traits are passed along in genes. Genes are special codes contained within all the cells of your body. They determine all of your inherited traits.

Traits such as eye color are carried in genes.

Biology is the science of life. Genetics is a part of biology that studies how traits are passed from one generation to the next. Genetics looks at the differences in genes between individuals and species. It can also help us answer questions about the history of life on Earth. Understanding genetics helps scientists figure out how to treat serious health problems. Genetics can even help solve crimes.

Studying Inheritance

Genetics is a new part of biology. Many of its discoveries have come only in the past century. But people have always noticed inheritance. Long ago they realized that individuals of one species have more in common with each other than with other species. It's easy to tell a giraffe from a hippo, even though they share some traits.

People also recognized that within a species, individuals show the same traits differently. Some cows make more milk than others. Some kinds of corn have sweeter kernels. Those traits are sometimes

Giraffes' long necks set them apart from most other species of mammals.

Inherited or Acquired?

Genes play an important role in determining how we look and behave. But they are not the only factor. Some traits are a combination of genes and environment. Your genes determine your height, but poor nutrition can limit your growth. If you don't like your hair color, you might dye it. Other traits are learned over time. Sports provide a good example. Kids are often introduced to sports by their parents or siblings. With practice, even a person who is not naturally talented can become successful.

passed down to offspring. Thousands of years ago, farmers began to choose the qualities they liked best. They bred plants and animals to produce sweeter corn, milk-rich cows, and more.

Scientists noticed that a similar process takes place in nature. In 1858 English scientists Charles Darwin and Alfred Russel Wallace described a process called natural selection. They noticed that some living things have traits well suited to their environment. These organisms are more likely to survive and reproduce. Over time, certain traits

Many of Darwin's insights came from observations he made aboard the ship HMS Beagle.

Darwin's Finches

In 1835 Darwin visited the Galápagos Islands west of the South American mainland. On every island he found similar-looking finches with differently shaped beaks. He noticed beak shapes were like tools. The beaks helped the birds reach their food. Insect eaters had long, thin beaks for reaching bugs inside trees. Seedeaters needed thick bills to crack shells. Darwin realized that long ago, a group of finches must have been blown from South America to the Galápagos. The survivors on each island were those with the beaks best suited to get the food on that island. In time, natural selection led to even better beaks. Fourteen species evolved from one ancestor.

become more or less common. This process, called evolution, gradually leads to new species.

Natural selection and evolution explained the great diversity of life on Earth. But a big question remained. How are traits passed from parents to children?

As a young man, Charles Darwin joined the crew of the HMS *Beagle* as the ship's naturalist. This is the last paragraph from Darwin's 1859 book on his observations during the journey:

> *It is interesting to contemplate an entangled bank, clothed with many plants of many kinds, with birds singing on the bushes, with various insects flitting about, and with worms crawling through the damp earth, and to reflect that these elaborately constructed forms, so different from each other, and dependent on each other in so complex a manner, have all been produced by laws acting around us. These laws [lead] to Natural Selection, entailing Divergence of Character and the Extinction of less-improved forms.*
>
> *Source: Charles Darwin.* On the Origin of Species (1859). *New York: Barnes & Noble Classics, 2004. Print. 384.*

What's the Big Idea?

Read this passage carefully. Ask an adult to help you look up any words you don't know. What was Darwin's main point about the natural laws that produce complex environments on our planet? Pick out two details he used to make this point. What can you tell about natural selection based on this paragraph?

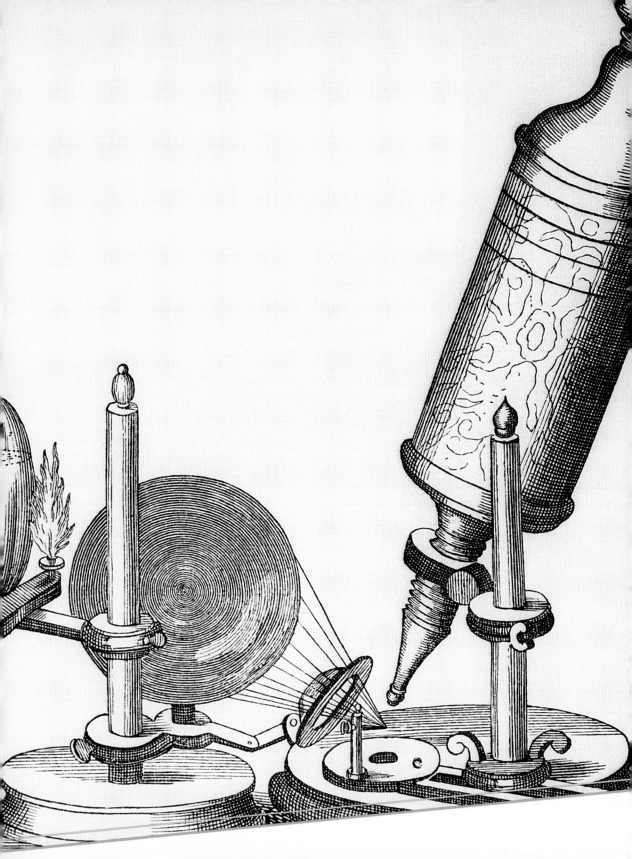

CHAPTER TWO

A SECRET IN THE CELLS

To early scientists, inheritance was a mystery. It took a long time to discover the clues and see how they all fit together. English biologist Robert Hooke found an important piece of the puzzle in 1665. In Hooke's time, microscopes weren't very useful. The lenses were poorly made. They produced blurry images. Hooke built his own microscope that made objects look 30 times larger. He also used

Robert Hooke discovered cells using his microscope, but he was unable to look at them closely enough to see the small features within them.

a special lamp to see under the microscope more clearly. He looked at many things, from fossils to insects. In the bark from a cork tree, he saw rows of tiny, hollow boxes. He called them cells. But he did not know the cells' purpose.

Mendel's Pea Plants

While Darwin and Wallace were studying natural selection, an Austrian monk named Gregor Mendel began his own work. He studied traits in pea plants. He noticed that simple traits such as seed color and shape were inherited by new generations. Mendel kept his plants in greenhouses to prevent insects from

Mendel's work with pea plants laid the groundwork for later genetic discoveries.

reaching them. He pollinated them by hand. This way, he knew the parents of each plant.

In one experiment, Mendel bred smooth-seeded peas with plants that had wrinkled seeds. He was surprised that all of the offspring had smooth seeds. When he bred the offspring to each other, the results changed. Now there were three smooth-seeded peas for every wrinkled one. He did similar tests for other traits. In every trait he tested, he found a ratio of approximately three to one.

Mendel concluded that each parent gives some inheritable material to the offspring. There are different forms of each trait. A parent could give either a dominant trait or a recessive trait. If at least one parent gives a dominant trait, the offspring will show the dominant trait. The offspring only shows the recessive trait if both parents give it the recessive trait. However, Mendel could not explain what this inheritable material was.

Powerful Microscopes

Higher-powered microscopes were invented in the 1800s. Scientists now had a close-up view of the natural world. In 1842 a Swiss plant biologist named Carl Nägeli observed long strands of material in a living cell. He called the strands chromosomes.

Twenty-seven years later, German scientist Walther Flemming invented a dye that more clearly revealed individual parts of the cell. Flemming watched as chromosomes unwound inside the nucleus at the center of the cell. Single chromosomes copied themselves. Then the copies formed pairs. Pairs lined up at the center of the cell. Next, they separated and went to opposite ends of the cell. Then the cell split in half. Now there were two cells, each containing a full and identical set of chromosomes. This process is called mitosis. It creates new cells to replace old or damaged ones.

Mendel had predicted that some material in the body transmitted traits from parents to offspring. Flemming's research showed that chromosomes might be that material.

Cells Come from Other Cells

American biologist Thomas Hunt Morgan began working with fruit flies in 1907. He bred the insects and observed the traits of each generation. One day Hunt noticed

The Living Cell
Living cells are filled with a jellylike material. Scattered within this material are many smaller parts. These are like the organs of the body. Each has a different job. One of the parts is the nucleus, which acts as the cell's brain.

something unusual. Among thousands of red-eyed flies was one with white eyes.

When Morgan bred this fly with a red-eyed fly, he got red-eyed offspring. Then Morgan bred the offspring's children. Just as Mendel had predicted, offspring of the second generation included flies with red eyes and flies with white eyes. There were approximately three red-eyed flies for each white-eyed one.

Morgan discovered male fruit flies were more likely than females to have white eyes. He knew that scientists had recently identified two chromosomes out of the full chromosome set that seemed to determine gender in animals. One was X-shaped. Another looked like a tiny letter Y. They are known as the sex chromosomes. In most species, including humans, females have two X chromosomes and males have one X and one Y chromosome. Morgan predicted that eye color is controlled by part of

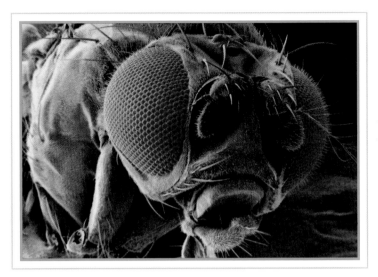

Fruit fly eye color was one of the traits that helped Morgan unlock the secrets of genetics.

the fruit fly's X chromosome. In other words, that chromosome holds a gene for that trait.

Morgan was right. Genes determine eye color and many other physical traits. The white fruit fly eye color is recessive. This means it must be present in all of a fly's X chromosomes in order to give the fly white eyes. Female flies have two X chromosomes, so they must receive the gene from both parents. Since male flies have just one X chromosome, they only need the gene from one parent. This made male flies more likely to have the white eye color. Morgan had built on the earlier work of many scientists and solved a mystery of inheritance.

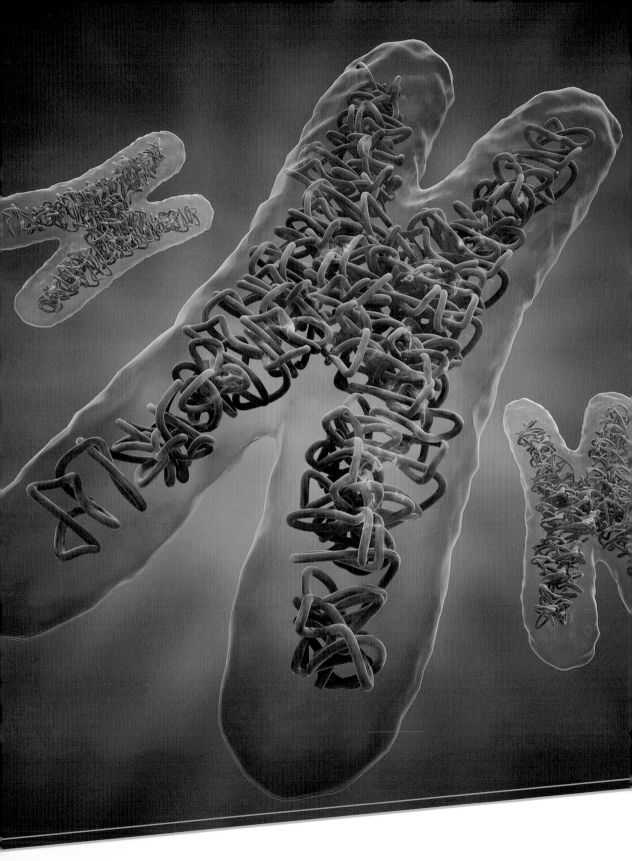

CHAPTER THREE

THE DNA CODE

What exactly is a chromosome? Imagine that someone gives you a very long piece of string. You could stretch the string out in a straight line or wad it up to hold it in one hand. It's the same amount of string. But when you squish it up, the string can fit in a smaller space. Chromosomes are extremely long molecules. They are made from deoxyribonucleic acid (DNA). Most of

Chromosomes are made up of tightly packed DNA strands.

the time, the DNA is packed into a small packet. This is a clever way to fit a lot of genetic material inside a small space.

The Structure of DNA

Scientists discovered the structure of DNA in the 1950s. British researchers Rosalind Franklin and Maurice Wilkins took pictures of DNA. Their work showed a ghostly X shape marked by dark stripes. This picture helped biologists James Watson and Francis Crick figure out the structure of DNA molecules. They built a model that looked like a long, spiraling ladder.

Each rung of the DNA molecule is made of two bases joined end to end.

Counting Chromosomes

Humans have 46 chromosomes arranged into 23 pairs. Chimpanzees are one of our closest animal relatives. These apes have 24 pairs of chromosomes and share 99 percent of our genes. *E. coli* bacteria, which live in the intestines of animals, have only one chromosome. At the other extreme, some ferns have up to 510 chromosome pairs.

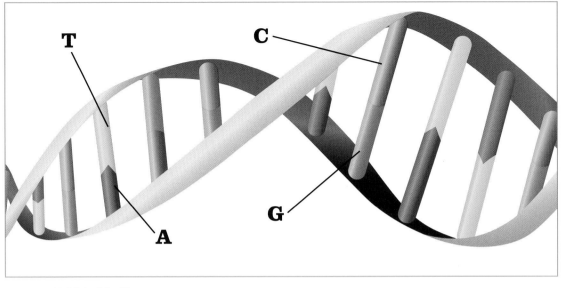

DNA Helix
This diagram shows the structure of DNA and the arrangement of the bases. After reading about this structure, how did you think it would look? Does this diagram surprise you?

Bases are made up of the chemical elements nitrogen, carbon, oxygen, and hydrogen. Four different bases make up DNA. Scientists abbreviate them as A, T, C, and G. A and T always match up. C always goes with G.

Genes are sections of DNA containing thousands of base pairs that work together. Each gene provides instructions for making a protein. Proteins help give the body its structure. They also carry out processes

Noncoding DNA

Only about 2 percent of human DNA is made up of genes. Between the genes are long stretches of DNA that scientists call noncoding DNA. Researchers are working to understand the purpose of these base pairs. Some think they might strengthen the long molecule. Others suspect they tell genes when and where to make proteins.

in the body. Several genes often work together to produce a single trait. Something as simple as the shape of your nose is the result of many genes.

Every cell in the body contains a complete copy of an organism's DNA. The exact sequence of base pairs in each organism's DNA is unique. However, parts of this code are the same in every living thing. This proves that all life on Earth has a common ancestor. The more similar the DNA is between two particular organisms, the more recently they had a common ancestor.

Scientists have long wondered how many genes we have and what they do. In 1990 many scientists around the world began working on the Human

Genome Project. A genome is the complete set of genes found in one set of chromosomes for a species. It has been called a library of the genetic code. The project, finished in 2003, has revealed that human DNA contains about 3 trillion base pairs and approximately 20,000 genes in each cell. By comparison, the genome of single-celled yeasts includes about 6,000 genes. Norway spruce trees have more than 28,000 genes.

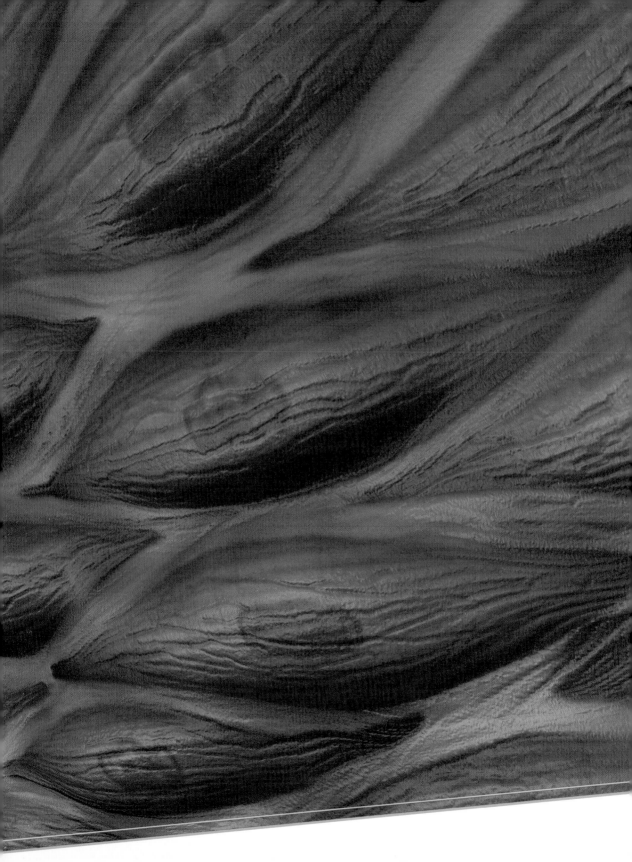

CHAPTER FOUR

NEW CELLS

Cells control all the functions needed for life. By the time you reach adulthood, your body will contain trillions of cells. Although each cell contains the same DNA, there are more than 200 different cell types. This is possible because genes within a particular cell can be turned off or on. For example, a cell that will become a muscle cell will have its genes for brain and bone cells turned off.

The contraction of muscle cells makes it possible for people to move.

The genetic code tells individual cells what to become and how to function. Cells work together to build muscle, skin, bone, and other parts of your body.

Mitosis and Meiosis

Mitosis is the process of cell division that allows organisms to grow and to replace old or damaged cells. Special cells are made for reproduction. These are the sex cells. Sex cells are different from body cells because they have half as many chromosomes. They are produced by another kind of cell division called meiosis.

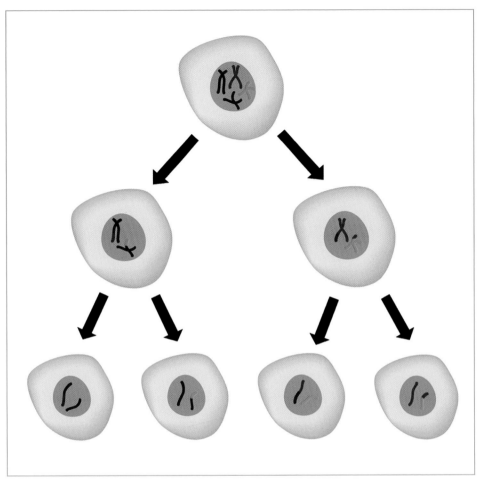

Meiosis
This graphic shows the stages of meiosis, including the chromosomes within the cells. How does this compare with your understanding of cell division from reading the text? How does it differ?

In meiosis, similar chromosomes pair up. Where they touch, the chromosomes may cross over and trade small pieces of DNA. As in mitosis, the chromosomes line up in the middle of the cell. Then the pairs split up. When the cell divides, each of the two new cells has one complete set of chromosomes. Then they divide again. The result is four sex cells, also called gametes. Human male and female gametes are known as sperm and eggs. Each contains one set of 23 chromosomes.

Offspring DNA

During reproduction, an egg from the mother combines with a sperm from the father. The new cell contains two sets of chromosomes. In humans, this provides the 23 pairs needed to make up the whole genome. The fertilized egg divides over and

---

Helpful Mutations

Harmful mutations can cause diseases. But many mutations are helpful. Think back to Darwin's finches on the Galápagos Islands. Mutations caused slight differences in beak shapes among the birds. Some could easily obtain food while others could not. Those helpful mutations were passed down from generation to generation. Over thousands of years, they led to the evolution of new species.

Identical twins make up approximately 3 out of every 1,000 births in the United States.

over again. The new cells start doing different jobs, eventually forming all the parts of a developing fetus. The same process takes place in species throughout nature.

Offspring look similar to their parents because they inherit DNA from both. But the process of meiosis gives children a slightly new combination of traits. Mutations can also influence the traits expressed by each individual. Mutations are like spelling errors. Just as words have different meanings when spelled incorrectly, genes behave in different

Mutations can result in unusually colored animals, such as blue lobsters.

ways after a mutation. Many mutations are harmless, causing no noticeable effects to the individual. Others can lead to diseases.

EXPLORE ONLINE

The Web site below provides more information about twins. You can learn new information from every resource. Reread Chapter Four of this book. How is the information provided on the Web site different from the information in this chapter? How do the two sources present information similarly? What can you learn from this Web site?

When You Are a Twin or Triplet
www.mycorelibrary.com/genetics

Sometimes a fertilized egg splits in two during its development. Two babies grow instead of one. They are identical twins. These children have exactly the same DNA in all their cells. Yet they won't behave or even look exactly alike. Both twins develop into unique people based on their lifestyles.

CHAPTER FIVE

PUTTING GENETICS TO USE

Genetics tells us about inheritance, but it can also be used to solve problems. Throughout history, people have suffered from diseases that could not be explained or predicted. Now we understand that mutations cause many diseases. For example, hemophilia is a disease in which the blood clots slowly. Cystic fibrosis is a genetic disorder that causes a person's body to make

The latest work on genetics can help save people's lives.

too much mucus. It clogs the lungs and upsets the digestive system. Genetic mutations cause both hemophilia and cystic fibrosis. Many genetic disorders such as these are recessive. Only people who inherit the gene from both parents have them.

There are many uses for genetic testing. Crime investigators can use it to solve cases. Doctors use genetic testing to identify disease-causing genes. These tests are sometimes done during pregnancy. Parents can learn in advance whether their child will face particular health risks. Adults may also choose genetic testing to make decisions about their own health care.

The Crime Scene

Genetic testing has become an important part of crime scene investigations. Blood, hair, and skin are among the DNA-containing substances found at crime scenes. By testing these samples, technicians can reveal the identity of victims or suspects. Using the same methods, a person can be proved innocent.

Genetically modified corn is better at resisting insects than natural corn.

Genetic Engineering

Scientists have learned some ways to make genes behave differently. This is called genetic engineering. One of the most common uses of this technology is in genetically modified (GM) foods. The first genetically engineered food was the Flavr Savr tomato. It was made available to the public in 1994. When normal tomatoes become too ripe, they grow mold that makes people sick. The Flavr Savr contained genes that stopped it from getting overripe. In GM foods, a new gene is inserted to replace part of the plant's genome. Some GM crops have new genome parts that protect against insects. Other foods could have vitamins added, making them more healthful.

Cloning is a kind of genetic engineering in which genetically identical organisms are made from parent cells. The first cloned animal was Dolly the sheep. She was grown in 1996 from a single cell, which came from an adult female sheep. Dolly lived for several years, stirring up excitement about the potential of cloning. Since 1996, scientists have cloned horses, dogs, cats, and other animals. No human beings have been cloned yet. Many people are opposed to trying to clone a person due to ethical issues.

Stem Cells

Certain kinds of cells can develop into any kind of tissue in the body. These are known as stem cells. They are found in the clump of dividing cells that grows a few days after fertilization. Some are also found in parts of the adult body. Someday, stem cells might be obtained from a patient's body and grown into whatever kind of cell the patient needs. For example, if a patient has a failing liver, his or her stem cells could create a new one.

Back from the Dead?

Extinction is a natural process that goes alongside evolution. Biologists calculate that on average through Earth's long history, between 10 and 100 species have gone extinct each year. Currently, the rate of extinction is much greater—about 27,000 species lost per year. Humans cause many of these extinctions by destroying natural habitats, polluting the air and water, and changing the climate. Some scientists suggest cloning extinct species using DNA from preserved bodies. The list of candidates includes familiar species that recently went extinct. It also includes animals that died out thousands of years ago, such as wooly mammoths.

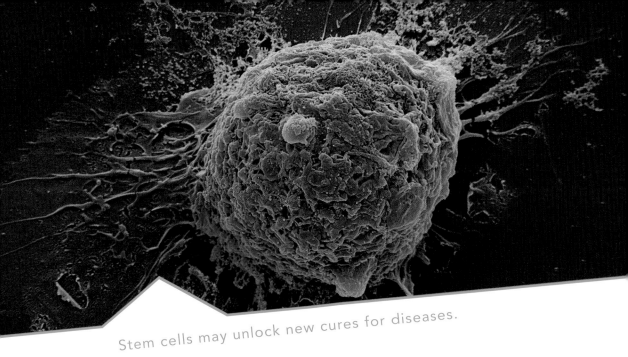
Stem cells may unlock new cures for diseases.

These uses of genetic science lead to questions about safety and ethics. Some people are concerned that genetically modified foods may not be healthful. They want these foods to be labeled so that consumers have a choice about what they eat. Most scientists agree that GM foods are safe. Another issue is cost. Examining a person's genes can be expensive. Will everyone benefit equally from advances in genetics research, or only the wealthy? By understanding genetics, you can make decisions about your own health and better appreciate the diverse world around us.

In 2013 US writer Stewart Brand discussed using DNA from museum specimens to bring back extinct species:

> *The Long Now Foundation is working on bringing back some extinct species, starting with the iconic passenger pigeon. Eventually the roster of revived species could include the woolly mammoth, the dazzling Carolina parakeet, the Tasmanian tiger (thylacine), the ivory-billed woodpecker, the great auk (penguin of the north seas), and hundreds of others. . . .*
>
> *It is becoming possible to take the DNA of extinct species in museum specimens and some fossils (no dinosaurs) and bring it back to life via the genomes of the closest living relatives of the extinct animals. Molecular biologists and conservation biologists are collaborating on ways to bring the creatures all the way back to where they belong—in the wild.*

Source: Stewart Brand. "I'm Speaking on De-extinction Next Tuesday." n.p., May 15, 2013. Web. Accessed May 15, 2013.

Changing Minds

Take a position on bringing back extinct species. Imagine that your best friend has the opposite opinion. Write a short speech trying to change your friend's mind. Make sure you explain your opinion and your reasons for it. Provide facts and details to support your reasoning.

Genetic Counselors

A genetic counselor works with people to identify their risk of inheriting diseases. Parents expecting a child often wish to know whether their baby is likely to have Down syndrome, spina bifida, or other health conditions. Adults may need to identify the cause of an existing health condition or want to know about future risks. Genetic counselors have an in-depth knowledge of inherited diseases and patterns of inheritance. Their job involves collecting a complete medical history, ordering and evaluating medical tests, and helping patients make decisions if they face a potential problem.

Genetic counselors can tell couples the chances of their child inheriting genetic conditions.

DNA at Crime Scenes

The forensic DNA analyst is an expert who helps to solve crimes and understand the cause of accidents. Most conduct DNA and chemical testing in police stations or government laboratories. This scientific evidence can prove the identity of a victim, or it may be used in court to provide evidence that a particular suspect was at the crime scene. DNA analysis has become an increasingly important part of modern police investigations.

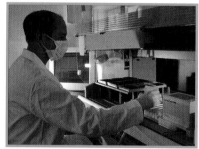

Hundreds of convicted people have been proven innocent by DNA testing.

DNA testing of grizzly bear hairs can give scientists a window into bear behavior.

Studying Grizzly Bear DNA

Wildlife biologists use genetic testing to learn about the genetic diversity of wild animals. DNA can reveal the relationships between individual animals in a population. It even helps biologists identify species. In Glacier National Park, researchers collected grizzly bear hairs. Using DNA analysis, they identified individual bears and learned how far individual bears traveled. This kind of information helps wildlife biologists better understand the lives of animals. Using genetics, biologists can also make more effective plans for conservation.

STOP AND THINK

Why Do I Care?

Many discoveries about genetics were made in the 1800s. That doesn't mean they are unimportant to modern science. How does the work of early geneticists such as Gregor Mendel and Thomas Hunt Morgan affect your life today? Are there technologies or services that might not exist without them? How might your life be different if these geneticists had never made their discoveries? Think creatively!

Say What?

You will always learn new vocabulary when studying science. Find five words in this book that are new to you. Use a dictionary or the glossary to learn the meanings of those words. Then define each term in your own words and use it in a new sentence.

Dig Deeper

After reading this book, what questions do you still have? Write down one or two questions that can guide you in doing research. With an adult's help, find a few reliable sources on genetics. Write a few sentences about your research.

Another View

This book had a lot of information about cells. Ask a librarian or other adult to help you find another source about cells. Write a short essay comparing and contrasting the new source's point of view with that in this book. What is the point of view in each source? How are they similar and different?

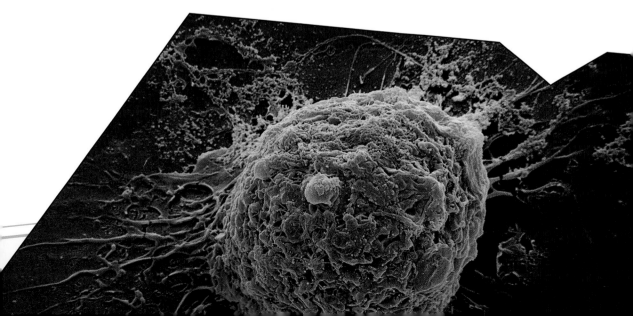

GLOSSARY

evolution
the gradual change in species over time

genome
the complete set of genes found in one set of chromosomes for a species

inherit
to receive something from a previous generation

mutation
a random change in a gene

nucleus
the part of a cell containing chromosomes

offspring
a parent's child or children

pollinate
to cause a process that lets plants reproduce

species
a group of organisms that are similar and can reproduce with each other

trait
a characteristic of an organism

LEARN MORE

Books

Hyde, Natalie. *Traits and Attributes*. New York: Crabtree Publishing Company, 2009.

Simpson, Kathleen. *Genetics: From DNA to Designer Dogs (National Geographic Investigates Science)*. Washington, DC: National Geographic, 2008.

Web Links

To learn more about genetics, visit ABDO Publishing Company online at **www.abdopublishing.com**. Web sites about genetics are featured on our Book Links page. These links are routinely monitored and updated to provide the most current information available.

Visit **www.mycorelibrary.com** for free additional tools for teachers and students.

INDEX

ABOUT THE AUTHOR

Before becoming a freelance writer, Christine Petersen enjoyed careers as a bat biologist and middle school science teacher. She has published more than 50 books for young people, covering topics in science, social studies, and health.